Rescuing the Declaration of Independence

How We Almost Lost the Words That Built America

Written by ANNA CROWLEY REDDING

Illustrated by EDWIN FOTHERINGHAM

HARPER

An Imprint of HarperCollinsPublishers

*N*ot long after revolutionary Americans battled the British to become the land of the free, America was at war with England once again.

And in 1814, as British ships sailed along the American coast, suspicions swirled in Washington that England wanted to humiliate the young country by burning its new capital to the ground.

SECRETARY OF STATE JAMES MONROE

had to know if the rumor was true—after all, he was one of the president's most trusted advisers. Monroe galloped toward a tiny town in Maryland. Perched atop a hill, he spied thousands of redcoats spilling out of enemy ships.

Their target was clear: *Washington.*

Monroe's heart sank. He knew the capital city was unprotected, undefended, unable to fight off an attack.

Grabbing a quill and paper, Monroe scribbled out two warnings, one for his clerk and one for President James Madison. And then he ordered a mounted soldier to rush those worrisome words to Washington as quickly as possible.

A cloud of dust followed the soldier as he raced through the sweltering August heat, down the streets of Washington to the White House, and then to the State Department in search of Monroe's office clerk.

STEPHEN PLEASONTON knew his boss was spying on the enemy. But he had *no* idea the British were coming. In fact, armed with a letter opener, Stephen was busy doing what he always did: reading notes, writing letters, organizing, and recording the recordables accordingly.

As a clerk, Stephen lived and breathed paper. His job was not a powerful post, but it came with a particularly spectacular perk!

If Stephen wanted to remember why America declared herself the land of the free, all he had to do was look up from his work. The *original* Declaration of Independence hung on the wall.

And if Stephen needed to defend his right to justice, liberty, and freedom of speech, why not grab a hold of the *original* U.S. Constitution and point to the perfect spot?

From the front door to the attic, his office was filled with George Washington's letters, the Bill of Rights, the Articles of Confederation, journals, and books—each piece of paper and parchment had a role in founding the country.

Yes, Stephen Pleasonton *knew* paper . . . but none of that prepared him for the urgent message from the front lines, delivered by a mounted soldier at full gallop.

The enemy is in full march for Washington.

Remove the records.

James Monroe,
Secretary of State
August 22, 1814

Holding the letter, Stephen's heart pounded. His eyes quickly scanned each line.

The last three words sent a chill down Stephen's spine.

"*Remove the records.*"

Stephen knew exactly which records his boss was talking about: the words that built America.

Stephen's mind raced as he faced the fact that he was standing between British torches and the greatest documents in the land.

In the name of *LIFE, LIBERTY, and the PURSUIT of HAPPINESS,* Stephen had to save them!

But how would he carry stacks of paper, reams of records, and bundles of books to safety? He needed bags and lots of them. **There was no time to waste!**

As the other two clerks prepared the paper for packing, Stephen bolted from the building to purchase fabric to be made into sturdy sacks.

Stephen stepped into the streets to find Washington erupting in chaos. News of the invasion was spreading fast. Militias gathered on the greens to prepare for battle. Stephen threaded through the crowded streets to the nearest shop.

Grabbing a bolt of coarse linen, he ran his hand over the material. This would be strong enough to carry America's ideas, beliefs, and rules of law to safety.

He ripped the cloth into large pieces while the merchant stitched them into sacks.

Seconds ticked by. Minutes. Hours. Then the last rip and the final stitch.

Stephen whisked the bags back to his office.

RIP!

Fingers bending and tucking, Stephen joined his fellow clerks as the men carefully rolled the documents into scrolls, working their way through three floors.

Surely, by now, the British were not far away. Stephen had to get those sacks out of town and fast! He needed wagons and lots of them. But from where? From whom?

Suddenly a booming voice froze Stephen where he stood. He found himself cornered by the secretary of war.

GENERAL JOHN ARMSTRONG was the most powerful military man in the country. He reported directly to the president.

The general demanded to know exactly what all the fuss was about. Stephen explained that the British were coming.

The general scoffed at the very notion of such silliness.

Ridiculous! Preposterous! Wrong!

In the general's not-so-humble opinion, he believed the British would never bother with Washington! After all, the capital was more pasture and swamp than grand government center.

The enemy is in full march for Washington.

Remove the records.

James Monroe,
Secretary of State
August 22, 1814

Even though there were big plans for
pleasing promenades, gorgeous gardens,
and astonishing architecture, at that very
moment, Washington was little more
than a beautiful city-to-be.

And once the general's mind was made
up, he would not budge an inch—
no matter what.

Stephen Pleasonton thought
about the documents he was
trusted to protect and
the British boots marching ever
closer. He may not have been
loud or rude, but when it came to
the safety of America's words, *he*
would not budge an inch, either.

The lowly clerk mustered whatever courage he could and *politely* told the general they would have to agree to disagree. Then Stephen stepped aside and **got back to work!**

As the general stormed off in a huff, Stephen hustled into the street once more to find transportation.

Dust hung in the air as fully loaded wagons jammed the roads. People were evacuating with as many possessions as they could carry.

Wading through the panicked crowd, Stephen began
to yell for help, **in the name of the United
States of America!**

He flagged down farmers, merchants, anyone with
a cart or wagon and convinced them to haul this
precious cargo safely out of town.

They lugged, lobbed, and lifted every last sack into
the wagons until they overflowed.

But where would the documents
be safe? Stephen remembered an
old gristmill, two miles north of
Georgetown. It was abandoned,
with plenty of room. And its thick
walls would surely keep these
national treasures safe.

With a snap of the reins, the
drivers were off.

Soaked in sweat, Stephen ran
back into his office for one last
look. Glancing around the room,
Stephen's eyes bulged.

They had missed one!

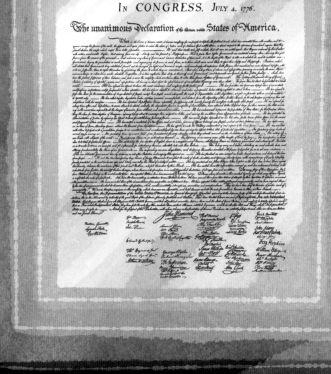

There, hanging proudly on the wall, was the

Declaration of Independence.

Of all the things to leave behind! Stephen pried the parchment from its frame and darted out the door.

Mounting his horse, Stephen raced into the night. Crossing the Potomac, he scanned every shadow, rock, and crevice for redcoats. But as he made his way to the mill, he realized he was galloping ever closer to another important building: a munitions factory!

It was a place where rifles, gunpowder, and cannons were made.
The perfect target for an attack. And it was only two miles from
the gristmill. If enemy troops targeted the factory, all it would
take was a spy or traitor to tip them off about the greatest trophy
of all—America's founding documents.

They were still in danger!

Stephen's horse's clattering hooves halted at the mill's front steps.
Body aching, bleary eyed, he stared at the massive pile of bags and
then at his exhausted coworkers.

There was no other choice. The documents had to be moved—again.
So, Stephen rode from farm to farm, calling out for help.

And again, everyday Americans came to the rescue.

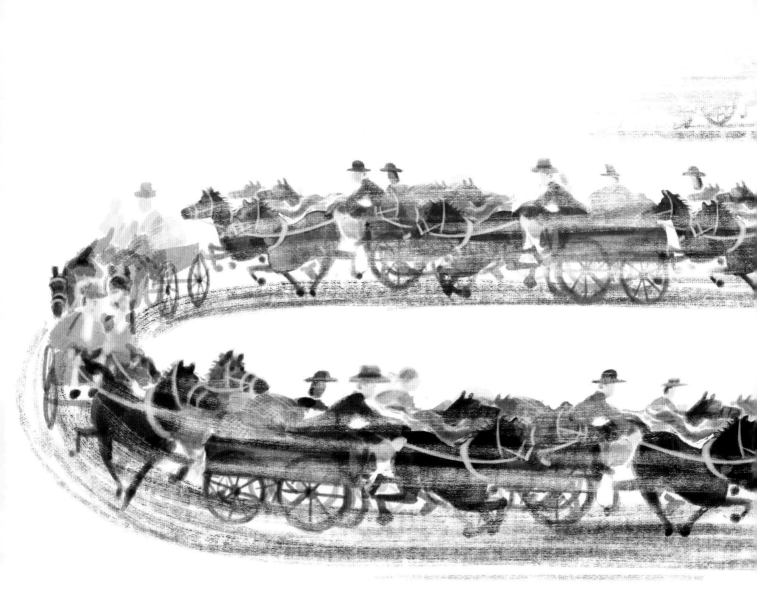

As the sun rose, Stephen led a train of wagons deeper into Virginia. After thirty-five long, bumpy miles, they rolled to a stop outside Leesburg, Virginia. A reverend brought them to an empty mansion with a brick vault. It was perfect. The documents would be safe there.

Hours later, after stashing sack after sack, Stephen's job was done. He closed the door and locked the mansion.

Ducking into the closest tavern, Stephen staggered into a guest room and collapsed onto the bed.

While he slept, an orange glow flickered on the horizon. **Washington was burning**. The White House, the Capitol, and Stephen's office were all ablaze.

Stephen would soon awake to the news that the **British seized Washington**. But while the redcoats destroyed the buildings, they did *not* erase the words that founded a nation.

When it was safe, Stephen Pleasonton would return those all-important words to Washington to shine as a guiding light.

In fact, if you need to remember why America declared herself the land of the free, you can read the *original* Declaration of Independence for yourself.

And should you need to defend your right to justice, liberty, and freedom of speech, you can inspect the *original* U.S. Constitution and point to the perfect spot.

All because an ordinary clerk did an extraordinary thing. While Stephen's heroic ride may have faded from memory, the words that built this country *never have and never will.*

AUTHOR'S NOTE

*I*magine my surprise to learn that the Declaration of Independence was nearly destroyed during the War of 1812! In all my history classes, from first grade to college, Stephen Pleasonton's amazing story was never told, taught, or otherwise talked about!

While standing in the National Lighthouse Museum in Rockland, Maine, I stumbled upon an exhibit about Pleasonton's heroic efforts to save our national treasures. I had to know more! Who was this forgotten hero? And so began my research into a government clerk with incredible courage.

General John Armstrong had more than a few confrontations with officials about his views on the likelihood of a British attack on Washington, even telling General John Peter Van Ness, "They certainly will not come here; what the devil will they do here?"

Why didn't Armstrong think Washington would be invaded? It was a brand-new capital in 1814. At the time, Baltimore was a far more important city. But the British chose Washington because they wanted to humiliate Americans by attacking and destroying the American seat of government. But Pleasonton stopped the British from getting the ultimate prize!

Although James Monroe's letter rallied Pleasonton to action, no one knows exactly what it said. But the one sent to the White House still exists, and its last line reads, "You had better remove the records." The note depicted in this book is inspired by that artifact.

After Pleasonton and his coworkers saved the documents from ruin, they remained in Leesburg for several weeks until it was safe to bring them back to Washington.

The documents had various homes over the next hundred and forty years. But in 1952, they finally made their way to the National Archives. Today the Declaration of Independence and the U.S. Constitution are protected by armed guards, alarms, and cameras. These documents are carefully preserved. (Archivists even pay attention to the temperature and humidity around them!) From time to time the documents have even needed repair. But most important, they still exist—thanks to Stephen.

As a reward for his service to our country, Stephen Pleasonton got a promotion to oversee the country's lighthouses, which is why there is an exhibit about him in Rockland!

The DECLARATION of INDEPENDENCE

Before the American Revolution, the United States of America did not exist. Instead our country was made up of thirteen colonies that belonged to the king of England.

But the colonists felt they were treated unfairly; for example, being taxed by the British government without having any representation. As tension built, the colonists decided it was time to become their own independent country, governed by the people.

The Declaration of Independence was drafted by a five-man committee that included Thomas Jefferson, John Adams, and Benjamin Franklin. Its most famous line boldly states, "We hold these truths to be self-evident, that all men are created equal, that they are endowed by their Creator with certain inalienable Rights, that among these are Life, Liberty, and the pursuit of Happiness.—That to secure these rights, Governments are instituted among Men, deriving their just powers from the consent of the governed."

As soon as the Declaration was ratified, on July 4, 1776, it was sent straight to the printer. These unsigned copies were quickly delivered by horseback to the thirteen states to get the word out to all in the land.

But America needed its own special copy, the official government record that would be held up as its rule of law and founding document. We needed a copy that would last.

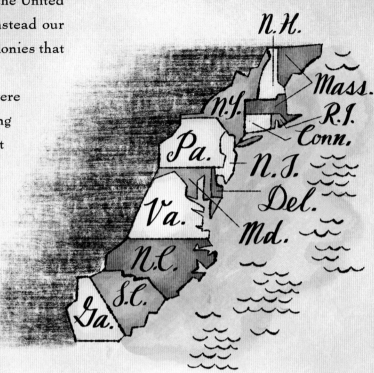

A man named Timothy Matlack, who had beautiful handwriting, sat down with a large piece of parchment, quill, and ink. His job was to engross (or handwrite) the *official* copy of the Declaration. He carefully looped letters, scripted sentences into perfectly straight lines, dotted *i*'s and crossed *t*'s. Copying the text word for word, he had to get it right. This piece of parchment would soon become America's official Declaration of Independence.

On August 2, 1776, the document was ready for signing. John Hancock was the first, followed by other members of Congress.

This official Declaration is the very one Stephen Pleasonton saved. And it is the very same document that you can still visit today.

The U.S. CONSTITUTION

*T*he Revolutionary War ended in 1783. The colonies were no longer colonies but actual *states*, part of the United States of America. However, just because the states were part of the same country did not mean they got along. In fact, they fought over everything from borders to taxes to laws.

Americans were especially nervous about giving the federal government too much power since they had just fought brutal battles to get rid of a king! Even so, things could not go on without some agreement on how the young country would actually function.

After lots of hard work and debate, the Constitution was signed on September 17, 1787.

Not only does the U.S. Constitution serve to protect citizens' rights, but it also lays out a plan for how the government works. It explains and dictates the roles of Congress, the Supreme Court, and even the office of the president.

The Bill of Rights includes the first ten amendments to the Constitution. They protect freedoms such as the right to worship the religion of your choice or to have no religion at all. Freedom of the press, the right to bear arms, and the right to speak your mind are just some of the freedoms covered by the Bill of Rights. These first ten amendments were adopted in 1791.

The ARTICLES of CONFEDERATION

*A*mong the many documents Stephen Pleasonton saved were the Articles of Confederation—known as America's first constitution. They were written during the Revolution. While these first documents helped to bring the country together, they didn't go far enough in making a strong country. That's why today we have the U.S. Constitution.

TIMELINE for the BURNING of WASHINGTON

August 22, 1814

Sec. of State James Monroe (who would later become president) spies the British army outside Washington, D.C. He pens a warning to the president and his clerk.

August 24, 1814

The British attack, torching the city and capturing America's new capital. Before setting fire to the White House, British soldiers sat at the dining room table inside and enjoyed a feast.

August 25, 1814

A powerful storm hits the capital. The British abandon Washington.

August 26, 1814

Stephen Pleasonton returns to the capital and finds his office building in ruins. The documents remained safely stashed in Virginia for weeks.

Want to see the documents Stephen Pleasonton saved?

Today, you can visit the Declaration of Independence, the U.S. Constitution, and the Bill of Rights. Collectively called the Charters of Freedom, these national treasures are carefully preserved and displayed at the National Archives Museum in Washington, D.C.

The museum is open seven days a week except for Thanksgiving and Christmas Day. Admission is free.

For more information, you may visit their website: www.archives.gov/museum/visit/reserved-visits.html.

You may also view the documents online anytime.

SELECTED BIBLIOGRAPHY

Herald and Torch Light. "Who Saved It." Hagerstown, MD. August 2, 1882: 1.

Ingraham, Edward D., and Peter Force. *A Sketch of the Events Which Preceded the Capture of Washington, by the British, on the Twenty-fourth of August 1814.* Philadelphia: Carey and Hart, 1849.

Kratz, Jessie. "The Burning of Washington." National Archives and Records Administration, August 18, 2014. https://prologue .blogs.archives.gov/2014/08/18/the-burning-of-washington/.

Kratz, Jessie. "P.S.: You Had Better Remove the Records: Early Federal Archives and the Burning of Washington during the War of 1812." *Prologue,* Summer 2014: 36–44. http://www.archives .gov/publications/prologue/2014/summer/1812.pdf.

Lusted, Marcia Amidon. *The U.S. Constitution.* Mankato, MN: Child's World, 2016.

Monroe, James. Memo from Secretary of State to the Speaker of the House of Representatives, November 14, 1814, in *American State Papers: Documents, Legislative and Executive, of the Congress of the United States,* vol. II: 252. Edited by Walter Lowrie and Walter S. Franklin. Washington, D.C.: Gales and Seaton, 1834.

Monroe, James. "Monroe to Madison." Letter to President James Madison. August 22, 1814. MS. National Archives, U.S. Representatives RG 233, Washington, D.C.

Pitch, Anthony S. "The Burning of Washington." The White House Historical Association. http://www.whitehousehistory .org/the-burning-of-washington.

U.S. National Archives and Records Administration. "The Declaration of Independence: A History." Accessed May 1, 2017, https://www.archives.gov/founding-docs/declaration-history.

Valley Falls New Era. "Saved a Famous MSS: How the Declaration of Independence Escaped." Valley Falls, KS. February 15, 1912: 1.

Van Ness, John Peter. Memorandum to U.S. Congress, November 23, 1814, in *American State Papers: Documents, Legislative and Executive of the Congress of the United States . . . Class V. Military Affairs,* vol. 1.: 580–583. Edited by Walter Lowrie and Matthew St. Clair Clarke. Washington, D.C.: Gales and Seaton, 1832.

To Quinn and Crowley—A.C.R.

For my family—E.F.

Rescuing the Declaration of Independence: How We Almost Lost the Words That Built America

Text copyright © 2020 by Anna Crowley Redding

Illustrations copyright © 2020 by Edwin Fotheringham

All rights reserved. Manufactured in China.

No part of this book may be used or reproduced in any manner whatsoever without written permission except in the case of brief quotations embodied in critical articles and reviews. For information address HarperCollins Children's Books, a division of HarperCollins Publishers, 195 Broadway, New York, NY 10007.

www.harpercollinschildrens.com

Library of Congress Control Number: 2018964880

ISBN 978-0-06-274032-8

The illustrations and hand lettering were drawn by hand on a digital device.

Typography by Molly Fehr

20 21 22 23 24 SCP 10 9 8 7 6 5 4 3 2 1

❖

First Edition